THE STRANGEST THING IN THE SEA

And Other Curious Creatures of the Deep

written by
RACHEL POLIQUIN

illustrated by
BYRON EGGENSCHWILER

KIDS CAN PRESS

For Beatrice and Henry — R.P.

For Truett — B.E.

Text © 2021 Rachel Poliquin
Illustrations © 2021 Byron Eggenschwiler

Published in Canada and the U.S. by Kids Can Press Ltd.
25 Dockside Drive, Toronto, ON M5A 0B5

Kids Can Press is a Corus Entertainment Inc. company

www.kidscanpress.com

The artwork in this book was made with scissors, construction paper, paints, colored pencils and a computer.
The text is set in HVD Bodedo and Times New Roman.

Edited by Yasemin Uçar and Olga Kidisevic
Designed by Andrew Dupuis

Printed and bound in Shenzhen, China, in 1/2023 by C & C Offset

CM 21 0 9 8 7 6 5 4 3

LIBRARY AND ARCHIVES CANADA CATALOGUING IN PUBLICATION

Title: The strangest thing in the sea : and other curious creatures of the deep / written by Rachel Poliquin ; illustrated by Byron Eggenschwiler.
Names: Poliquin, Rachel, 1975– author. | Eggenschwiler, Byron, illustrator.
Identifiers: Canadiana 20200366661 | ISBN 9781771389181 (hardcover)
Subjects: LCSH: Marine animals — Juvenile literature.
Classification: LCC QL122.2 .P65 2021 | DDC j591.77 — dc23

Kids Can Press gratefully acknowledges that the land on which our office is located is the traditional territory of many nations,
including the Mississaugas of the Credit, the Anishnabeg, the Chippewa, the Haudenosaunee and the Wendat peoples, and is
now home to many diverse First Nations, Inuit and Métis peoples.

We thank the Government of Ontario, through Ontario Creates; the Ontario Arts Council; the Canada Council for the Arts;
and the Government of Canada for supporting our publishing activity.

The seas are filled with strangeness.

Dancing feathers. Goblin teeth. See-through heads.
Creatures that seem to be made from stardust.

Some animals carry lanterns to light their way …
or is it to lure their victims through the darkness?
Some seem to be rocks, but rocks don't swallow
their dinners whole … or do they? Not everything
is quite as it seems.

The seas are filled with strangeness. But what is
the strangest thing of all?

I look like a silvery moon
with graceful wings.
Some people call me the
Swimming Head.

Am I the strangest thing
in the sea?

I am long, soft and
ghostly. My nose is
pointed like a witch's,
and my teeth are
downright spooky.

Am I the strangest thing in the sea?

The sunfish's huge dorsal fin is often mistaken for a shark's fin.

Pieces of kelp forests sometimes break off and float out to sea. These kelp paddies give creatures shade and landing pads in the open ocean. They often become cleaning stations where sunfish come to have parasites bitten off by seagulls and cleaner fishes.

Females can lay an astonishing 300 000 000 eggs at once! Once they hatch, the tiny fry (recently hatched fish) look like floating stars.

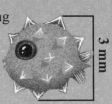

3 mm

I'M AN OCEAN SUNFISH

I really am a swimming head. My backbone is shorter than your pinky finger, and I don't have a tail like most fish — it's more of a frilly rudder to keep me swimming straight.

I dive down deep to eat jellyfish. Nobody eats jellyfish like me — I can eat over half my weight in jellyfish a day. I eat enough to grow big, bigger, HUGE. I start life smaller than a grain of rice and grow 60 million times bigger! We sunfish are the heaviest bony fish in the sea. We can weigh over 2000 kg (4400 lb.) and grow as tall as an elephant!

I love to sunbathe at the surface to warm myself. Floating also lets seagulls and cleaner fishes nip away all my pests and parasites. I am covered with thousands of pests. Nasty nuisances — they are always biting me!

I'm a giant floating fish head, but I'm not the strangest thing in the sea.

SIZE: up to 3.5 m (11.5 ft.) long
PREY: jellyfish, fish, squid and crustaceans
HABITAT: warm open waters around the globe
DEPTH: surface to 800 m (2625 ft.)

I'M A
GOBLIN SHARK

I'm named for a long-nosed goblin from Japanese folktales: *tengu*.
My snout is even longer than his, and my mouth has a truly nasty
surprise. At dinnertime, my jaws lunge forward — right out of my
head! My needle teeth stab the fish, then my jaws snap back like
a slingshot.

I live down deep where the ocean is dark and life is slow. I'm not
fast or sleek, like some sharks. I'm flabby. I dawdle. A few soft
swishes of my long tail get me to most places I need to go.

I like to float, quietly waiting for a fish or squid to come close.
My eyes are small and the waters are dark, but my snout can sense
the tiniest electric fields produced by all living things. It knows
when dinner is near.

I am a fanged and flabby goblin, but I'm not the strangest thing
in the sea.

SIZE: 3.6 m (12 ft.) long
PREY: fish, squid, crustaceans and octopus
HABITAT: oceans and seas worldwide but most
        frequently sighted in waters around Japan
DEPTH: 300 m to at least 1300 m (984–4265 ft.)

The goblin shark's skin is see-through and looks pink because of blood vessels just under the skin.

Thin, needle-like teeth don't fit into the goblin shark's mouth, even when its jaws are closed.

It's important to save energy in the deep ocean — it's dark and cold, the pressure of the water is heavy, and food can be hard to find. The goblin shark's flabby body helps it float, and swimming slowly saves energy

I look like a tiptoeing
rock wearing a wig.
I even have a bow in
my hair, sort of.

Am I the strangest thing in the sea?

I'M A YETI CRAB

I'm called a yeti crab because I'm hairy and white, like the yeti, that legendary mountain monster. The yeti is said to have white fur to stay warm and blend in with snow. I'm white (and blind!) because I live in total darkness at the bottom of the ocean — no need for fancy colors or eyes down here! And I'm hairy because I'm a farmer. Let me explain.

I live with my fellow yetis on a hydrothermal vent — an underwater volcano that grows from a crack in the ocean floor. The hot vent spews out boiling water, chemicals and gases, which help me farm my dinner … right on my body!

You see, my fur-like bristles are covered with bacteria. These tiny creatures usually need energy from the sun to survive. There's no sunlight down here, but my bacteria can make energy from the chemicals in the boiling water. I wave my claws near the hot vents to feed the bacteria on my body, then I gobble the bacteria up. It's weird, but it works.

I'm a blind and hairy farmer on a boiling volcano, but I'm not the strangest thing in the sea.

The first species of yeti crab was discovered in 2005 by marine biologists in a submarine while they were exploring hydrothermal vents in the deep South Pacific Ocean.

SIZE: 15 cm (6 in.) long
PREY: bacteria
HABITAT: deep-sea hydrothermal vents
DEPTH: 2400 m (7875 ft.)

Without energy from the sun, deep-sea bacteria and other tiny microbes make energy from the chemicals — such as hydrogen sulfide — spewed out from hydrothermal vents in a process called chemosynthesis.

The deep sea is always cold, but one species of yeti crab lives in the especially cold deep sea near Antarctica. The freezing waters can paralyze the crabs, so they cram around the hot hydrothermal vents for warmth — as many as 600 crabs in 1 square meter (10 square feet)!

I look like a dancing tutu.
Graceful as a ballerina,
I flutter my feathers up
and down, up and down, as
I swan through the water.

Am I the strangest thing
in the sea?

I'M A
FEATHER STAR

I look like a feathery plant, but I am an animal, just like you.

I swim by waving my "feathers" up and down. My feathers are actually arms, which have thousands of tiny, sticky tube feet that are always waving and wiggling to catch plankton or other tiny, tasty things floating by. When a foot snags something, it passes it to the next foot, which passes it to the next foot, like a conveyor belt, all the way to my mouth at the center.

I start out life with five arms. But if I lose one, I can grow two in its place. Imagine if you could do that! The new arms might take nine months to grow, but I can grow as many as 200 in a lifetime. The more I grow, the heavier I get. If I'm too heavy to swim, I stroll along the ocean floor. Sometimes I pretend to be a plant and grip onto rocks and corals with my clawlike legs.

I'm a dancing bouquet of hungry feathers, but I'm not the strangest thing in the sea.

Feather stars don't have many predators, but sea urchins love them. If an urchin catches an arm, the feather star drops it and runs away at a top speed of 5 cm (2 in.) per second, which is very slow, but faster than an urchin!

SIZE: up to 0.6 m (2 ft.) wide
PREY: plankton and tiny particles
HABITAT: most common in shallow, warm waters in the Indo-Pacific Ocean, but widely distributed
DEPTH: surface to 1500 m (4921 ft.) or deeper (depending on the species)

Feather stars look feathery, but they are mostly made of calcium carbonate, the same material as eggshells.

A feather star's mouth is at the center of its body. It has a U-shaped gut, which means its mouth is right next to its bum.

I'm a glowing village of tiny creatures, all decorated with lights. Together we sparkle in the darkness. Even our village bell glows.

Am I the strangest thing in the sea?

I'M A
GIANT SIPHONOPHORE

Look at me! Aren't I dazzling? But I'm not just one me. I'm thousands of me's all living together in a giant colony of clones.

We are called a siphonophore. That's a long name, so let us help: say sai-FAA-nuh-for. We grow by cloning more of us to add to the chain. Together we might stretch 40 m (130 ft.) — that's longer than a blue whale! Imagine if a blue whale was made of thousands of tiny blue whales, each doing its own special job. That's how we work — some of us swim, some catch food, some eat it, some sting. We are individual creatures, but none of us could live alone.

We charm fish and jellies with our glowing tentacles, then sting them dead. And if we bump something, our long, thin body glows blue.

But remember, we don't really have one long body — there are thousands of us living as one. And that dome isn't a head — it's a float that keeps us at exactly the right depth.

We're a twinkling family of deadly stingers, but we're not the strangest thing in the sea.

SIZE: up to 40 m (130 ft.) long
PREY: small crustaceans, jellyfish and fish
HABITAT: deep seas
DEPTH: 700–1000 m (2297–3281 ft.)

Most siphonophores live in the deep sea where the weight of the water is enormous. The water's pressure on their bodies actually holds the colonies together. Most siphonophores would burst if they came to the surface.

The giant siphonophore's tentacles are covered in stingers called nematocysts. They shoot tiny barbs filled with venom into anything they touch.

The Portuguese man-of-war is the most famous siphonophore, although people often mistake it for a jellyfish. It doesn't live in the deep sea like most siphonophores, but bobs on the surface with its jelly float.

I have a cloak of fleshy
spines and giant red eyes.
I'm named for a fanged
monster of the night.

Am I the strangest thing
in the sea?

I'M A
VAMPIRE SQUID

I look scary, but I'm actually gentle and a bit shy. When frightened, I pull my cloak-like webbing right over my head and turn into a spiky ball. Or I might shoot a sticky cloud of glowing goo to hide my escape.

I spend most of my time deep, deep down in total darkness. That's why my eyes are so big — to catch the faintest flickers from other animals. I also have my own lights that I sometimes flash and blink to confuse predators in the dark.

I drift, slowly flapping my two fins while two long strings float behind me. These strings catch tiny specks of dead animals and plants falling from above. It's called marine snow, and it's what I eat. See? I'm not really a scary monster! I won't hurt anyone.

I'm a cloaked and stealthy dweller of the dark, but I'm not the strangest thing in the sea.

SIZE: 15–30 cm (6–12 in.) long
PREY: marine snow
HABITAT: temperate and tropical oceans
DEPTH: 300–3000 m (984–9843 ft.)

Vampire squid live in deep, slow-moving water with almost no oxygen. Most animals would die here, but vampire squid have evolved to thrive in these zones.

Very little sunlight reaches the deep ocean, and red light in particular is quickly filtered out. That means red animals, such as vampire squid, are near invisible in the dark ocean waters.

Vampire squid have eight arms like an octopus, yet they are neither squid nor octopuses, but an ancient relative. Scientists call them living fossils because they have barely changed over 200 million years.

I live in a land of candy balls.
My home is covered in candy
balls. I'm covered in candy balls.
Even my friends are covered in
candy balls.

Am I the strangest thing in the sea?

I'M A
PYGMY SEAHORSE

Look how cute I am! I'm the size of your thumbnail, and I spend my entire life on a small part of this sea fan — it's a kind of coral, and it's exactly 100 percent as cute as I am. Can you even tell us apart?

I'm a pink pygmy seahorse, so I live on a pink sea fan. But I have orange cousins on orange sea fans, purple cousins on purple sea fans, and you'd never know any of us are here. Camouflage is very important because we're so dainty. Plus, we're the slowest fish in the sea. We can move only around 1.5 m (5 ft.) per hour. That's slower than a snail.

But who needs to go anywhere? My friends live close by, and the ocean currents bring me brine shrimp and other tiny nibbles. I just have to hold on tight with my long, strong, curly tail, or the currents would carry me away, too!

I'm the tiniest, pinkest, sweetest candy-ball horse, but I'm not the strangest thing in the sea.

Pygmy seahorses are one of the few species of seahorses that live closely together. As many as twenty adults might live in a small cluster on the same sea fan.

SIZE: usually less than 2 cm (0.8 in.) long
PREY: tiny crustaceans, such as brine shrimp
HABITAT: warm coastal waters through Southeast Asia, from southern Japan to Australia
DEPTH: 10–40 m (33–130 ft.)

Like all corals, a sea fan is a cluster of tiny animals living together. Each warty knob is an individual animal called a polyp, and each has starlike tentacles for catching its own food.

Pygmy seahorses are so tiny and well camouflaged, no one knew they existed until 1969 when they were accidentally discovered on a piece of coral taken into a laboratory.

I look like a fighter jet.
When I'm young, I fly
between the trees. And I
always carry my chainsaw
with me.

Am I the strangest thing in the sea?

I look like an angel
floating in a glittering
constellation of stars.

Am I the strangest thing
in the sea?

Mangroves are the only trees able to grow in salt water. Their tangle of roots and secret underwater forests make the perfect hiding spot for young sawfish.

The largetooth sawfish has between fourteen and twenty-four denticles. They grow throughout the fish's life, but if lost, they don't grow back.

Sawfish are among the most threatened fish in the world. Their fins are used in shark-fin soup. Their long-toothed snouts are used in traditional medicines or sold as collectibles.

I'M A LARGETOOTH SAWFISH

Nothing about me is quite as it seems. My chainsaw isn't a nose — it's part of my skull. My saw-teeth aren't teeth — they're special scales called denticles. My lips are covered in hundreds of hard, tiny bumps which are my actual teeth. And while I look like a shark, I'm really a ray.

You might guess I use my saw as a sword to defend myself or slash fish for dinner, and you're right. But my saw also has invisible powers. I live in the shallow waters around estuaries where rivers meet the sea. The waters here can be murky, but my saw can sense a fish's tiniest haze of electricity in the cloudiest water.

I spend my early years among the mangrove forests, and sometimes travel far upriver. But I always come back to the sea, and spend my adult life in warm, shallow waters along the coast.

I have a saw with a sixth sense, but I'm not the strangest thing in the sea.

SIZE: up to 7 m (23 ft.) long
PREY: fish, prawns and other crustaceans
HABITAT: warm, shallow waters including estuaries, rivers and lakes
DEPTH: up to 25 m (82 ft.), but usually less than 10 m (33 ft.)

Can rainbows walk? This one can.
Do rainbows see better than you?
You better believe it. I even have
a pair of boxing gloves, and I'm
not afraid to use them.

Am I the strangest thing in the sea?

Clogged houses are packed with food bits. Once they are dumped, the houses sink, bringing valuable food down to creatures living in deeper waters.

Giant larvaceans build a new house every day or so. After they dump their houses, they just swim away and start building again.

Smaller larvaceans build small houses, sometimes only 2.5 cm (1 in.) wide, and can replace them hourly.

I'M A
GIANT LARVACEAN

Most of what you see is my house. I'm the tadpole-like creature in the middle of the beautiful "wings."

I'm a tunicate, which means I don't have a single bone in my body. Most tunicates are rooted in one place, but not me. I swim wherever I want. And wherever I go, I bring my house.

Scientists call it a house, but it's really a fishing net. I eat very, very tiny bits of food falling from above. My outer net traps bits too big for me to eat — those are the "stars" in my constellation. Inside, my angel wings are delicate filters guiding the tiniest bits into my mouth. I keep the water (and food) flowing through my filters by always pumping my tail.

My house is beautiful, but it's made of sticky mucus and gets clogged and heavy. When it does, I kick off the whole thing — the house and my angel-wing filters — and start building again.

I'm a sticky angel in a starry house, but I'm not the strangest thing in the sea.

SIZE: 10 cm (4 in.) long, but their houses can
      be more than 1 m (3 ft.) wide
PREY: marine snow
HABITAT: mid-waters throughout the world
DEPTH: 90–275 m (295–2953 ft.)

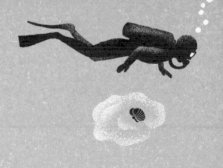

I look like an alien spaceship with kissy lips. If that weren't weird enough, you can see what might be two green aliens inside ... because my head is *see-through*! You can actually see *inside* my head!

Am I the strangest thing in the sea?

Scientists don't understand exactly how these strange eyes work, but they think mantis shrimp may process images very quickly inside their eyeballs without having to send much information to their brains — which is good, because their brains are very small.

With such a powerful punch, why don't the clubs break? It's because their fibers are arranged in a unique spiraling herringbone pattern. This same pattern is used to design super-strong materials for airplanes and body armor.

I'M A PEACOCK MANTIS SHRIMP

Rainbow explosion! Have you ever seen anything like me?

Let's start at the top. Those two round balls are my eyes, and they're the best eyeballs around. For starters, I have trinocular vision *in each eye*! With your two eyes together, you only have binocular vision, which means I see better than you even with one eye closed! I have four or five times more color receptors than you and can see things you can't even imagine. And I can move each eyeball independently — so, quite literally, I SEE EVERYTHING.

Then there's my punch. I'll smash anything that comes my way. My clubs can break clams or pulverize crabs. I could split your thumb open to the bone or even shatter aquarium glass! My punch is as fast as a speeding bullet. It's the hardest punch in the animal kingdom.

I am a violent rainbow boxer, but I'm not the strangest thing in the sea.

Mantis shrimp hide in crevices and burrows on the ocean floor and among corals. They are very territorial and attack anything that comes close.

SIZE: 10–15 cm (4–6 in.) long
PREY: fish, crustaceans and worms
HABITAT: warm waters of the Indian and Pacific Oceans
DEPTH: 3–40 m (10–130 ft.)

I'm a shape-shifter. In sunlit waters, I am long and sleek as a seal. But when I sink deeper into darker waters, I grow an enormous, unbreakable shell with flashing lights.

Am I the strangest thing in the sea?

These green blobs are the lens in the
fish's eyes. The green color may filter
out sunlight to better see the glow from
bioluminescent animals.

Large fins allow barreleye fish
to stay motionless in the water,
for extra-sneaky attacks.

Barreleye fish have excellent binocular vision for
judging depth, and tracking and attacking prey.
But they aren't so good at looking sideways.

I'M A
BARRELEYE FISH

I'm even stranger than I look. Those black circles aren't my eyes. They're my nostrils. My real eyes are the two green alien-like blobs inside my head.

I live in deep, dark waters. My eyes usually point straight up — through the top of my head! — and they are very good at seeing the faintest shadows and flickers of motion above me. They're especially good at telling the difference between sunlight and the glowing lights from bioluminescent animals.

I hover in darkness, just below where sunlight reaches. When I see a flash of something tasty above, I swivel and swim straight up to get it. Sometimes I steal dinner from nasty stinging siphonophores — their tentacles glow when a jelly or fish knocks into them, and I can see their light. The siphonophore would sting and blister my eyes if it could, but with my see-through head, I can steal dinner with my eyes open and not get burned at all.

I'm a sneaky thief with aliens in my head, but I'm not the strangest thing in the sea.

SIZE: 15 cm (6 in.) long
PREY: jellyfish, fish and zooplankton
HABITAT: North Pacific Ocean
DEPTH: 600 m (1969 ft.) and deeper

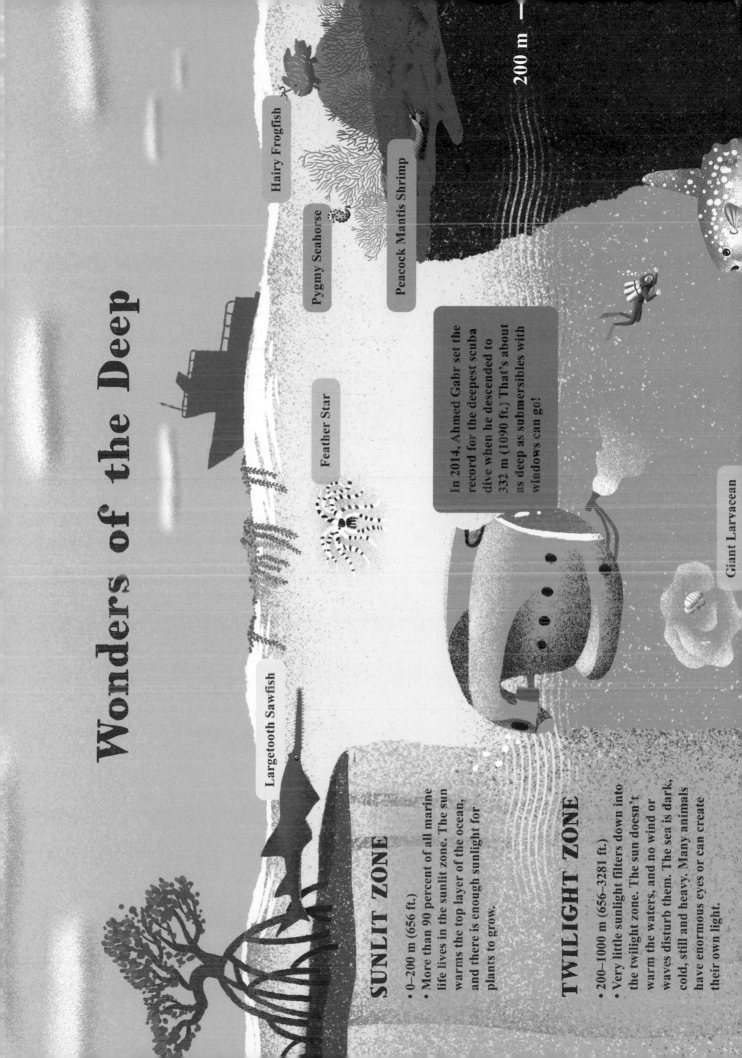

Wonders of the Deep

200 m

Hairy Frogfish

Pygmy Seahorse

Peacock Mantis Shrimp

Feather Star

In 2014, Ahmed Gabr set the record for the deepest scuba dive when he descended to 332 m (1090 ft.) That's about as deep as submersibles with windows can go!

Largetooth Sawfish

Giant Larvacean

SUNLIT ZONE

- 0–200 m (656 ft.)
- More than 90 percent of all marine life lives in the sunlit zone. The sun warms the top layer of the ocean, and there is enough sunlight for plants to grow.

TWILIGHT ZONE

- 200–1000 m (656–3281 ft.)
- Very little sunlight filters down into the twilight zone. The sun doesn't warm the waters, and no wind or waves disturb them. The sea is dark, cold, still and heavy. Many animals have enormous eyes or can create their own light.

Most of Earth's surface is underwater, and scientists estimate that around 80 percent of the oceans are still unmapped and unexplored. Imagine what new and wonderful strangeness lurks in those unknown waters!

Few scuba divers go deeper than 40 m (130 ft.) or about the depth of a ten-story building. Any deeper, and the weight of the water can make divers dizzy and weak. Divers can die if they come up too quickly.

I'M AN OCEAN EXPLORER

Under the waves, I'm the oddest of creatures. I can't breathe. I don't swim particularly well. I can't even go much beyond the shallows without becoming sick. But that doesn't stop me from transforming into ever-new shapes and forms to discover worlds beneath the waves.

I've made fins to help me swim, and thick, skin-like suits to keep me warm. I carry my oxygen in tanks and bring flashlights and weights to help navigate waters that any fish could swim with ease. And all of this still only lets me explore the ocean's topmost layer — there is so much more below!

Most of the sea is kilometers deep — so vast and full of life, and I am so curious! But the waters quickly become impossibly cold, dark and heavy. They would freeze and crush me. So I've built thick-walled submarines and underwater robots to help me explore the wonders of the deep.

I am a shape-shifting explorer of unknown worlds, but I can't survive underwater without tools and inventions. Am I the strangest thing in the sea? I think so, but you tell me!

The *Alvin*, a deep-ocean research submersible, fits three people and has lights, video cameras and two robotic arms. It can descend to 4500 m (14 763 ft.).

GLOSSARY

bacteria: tiny living organisms that are made up of a single cell

barb: a sharp, curved point, such as a thorn or fishhook

binocular vision: a type of vision in which both eyes are used at the same time to create a single image

bioluminescence [bye-oh-loo-mee-NES-uhns]: a living creature's ability to make light biologically

camouflage: the ability of some animals to disguise their appearance and blend into the background

chemosynthesis [KEE-moh-SIN-thuh-sis]: the process by which food is produced using the energy released by chemical reactions

cleaning station: a place where aquatic animals come to be cleaned by other animals

clone: to make an exact copy of a living thing by copying its genetic information

color receptors: special parts of the eye that are able to absorb different parts of the light spectrum

constellation: a group of stars that appear to form a pattern when viewed from Earth

crustacean [kruh-STAY-shun]: an animal, such as a crab, lobster or shrimp, with a hard shell and several pairs of legs. Crustaceans usually live in water.

denticle: a small tooth or toothlike projection

digestive juices: liquids created by the digestive sytem to break food down into nutrients

dorsal fin: found on the back of most fish, this fin helps with stabilization and sharp turns. Great white sharks have famous dorsal fins.

ecosystem: a biological community of living and non-living things

electric field: the electrically charged area produced by and surrounding an electrically charged object

estuary [ES-choo-air-ee]: an area at the mouth of a river where seawater and freshwater meet

habitat: the natural home or environment of an animal, plant or other organism

hydrothermal vent: a crack in the ocean floor from which boiling water (heated inside the Earth) spews out

kelp paddy: a floating chunk of kelp

living fossil: a living creature, such as a turtle or horseshoe crab, that closely resembles its ancient ancestors

marine snow: bits of dead animals, skin flakes, poop and other organic matter that drift downward through the ocean like little snowflakes

nematocyst [NEM-uh-tuh-sist]: a special cell that shoots out a venom-filled barb when touched

parasite: a small organism that lives on or inside another living thing, often causing it harm or pain

plankton: tiny plants and animals that float with the oceans' currents

polyp [POL-ip]: a small creature, such as coral or a sea anemone, whose body is attached to a surface at one end

submersible: a vehicle designed for underwater exploration and research

swim bladder: an internal gas-filled organ that helps fish swim and control their depth

tengu: a creature from Japanese folklore with a long nose and an angry red face

trinocular vision: a type of vision in which each eye moves, sees and gauges depth independently. The only known animal with this type of vision is the mantis shrimp, who has the ability to focus three parts of one eye on one object to create a single image.

tunicate [TOO-ni-kit]: barrel-shaped animals that feed on plankton by filtering it from the water they suck into and squirt out of their bodies

venom: a poisonous substance secreted by some animals and usually injected by biting or stinging

yeti: a large, hairy humanlike creature said to live in the Himalayan Mountains

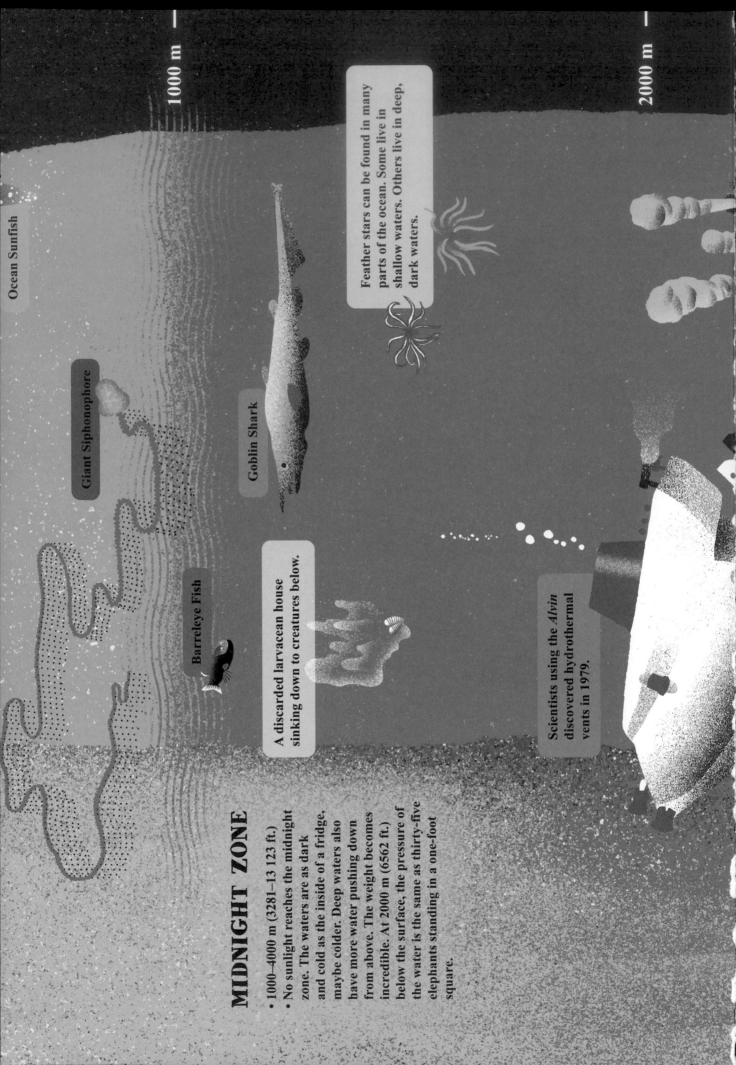

Ocean Sunfish

— 1000 m

— 2000 m

Feather stars can be found in many parts of the ocean. Some live in shallow waters. Others live in deep, dark waters.

Giant Siphonophore

Goblin Shark

Barreleye Fish

A discarded larvacean house sinking down to creatures below.

Scientists using the *Alvin* discovered hydrothermal vents in 1979.

MIDNIGHT ZONE

- 1000–4000 m (3281–13 123 ft.)
- No sunlight reaches the midnight zone. The waters are as dark and cold as the inside of a fridge, maybe colder. Deep waters also have more water pushing down from above. The weight becomes incredible. At 2000 m (6562 ft.) below the surface, the pressure of the water is the same as thirty-five elephants standing in a one-foot square.

3000 m —

Hydrothermal Vent

Yeti Crab

Vampire Squid

The deepest known part of the ocean
is the Challenger Deep in the Pacific
Ocean. It is 11 km (almost 7 mi.) deep.
In order to show its bottom, this page
would need to be three times as long!

In 1960, Jacques Piccard and Don
Walsh were the first people to visit
the Challenger Deep in a submersible
named *Trieste*.

TO THE ABYSS

• 4000–6000 m (13 123–19 685 ft.)
• Descending further into the
abyss, the waters become
ever colder and their pressure
continues to increase. Yet
amazingly, these waters are still
full of life.

The seas are home to dozens of unique habitats, each as different from the other as deserts are from rain forests. Coral reefs. Mangrove forests. Hydrothermal vents. The deep, dark depths of the abyss. Each are filled with creatures so beautifully adapted to their particular waters, they could not live anywhere else.

Open the flap to see and learn more about the fascinating worlds under the sea.